Would You Like to Hear a Happy Story?

WAYNE ANDERSON

ISBN-13: 9780986317835
First Edition: 2018

10 9 8 7 6 5 4 3 2 1

Cover Photo: Michael Simmons©123RF.com

CONTENTS

.

FOREWORD

My reason for writing this book is to help those who are incarcerated understand addiction and recidivism coming from one of their own rather than a psychologist or drug counselor who has never experienced either. It is also my hope to shed light and insight into how we might be able to overcome both.

However, my sole purpose is to not only assist and guide or redirect a large percentage of the prison population in the direction that is needed to overcome our addictions, but also for those that fear the risk of recidivating upon their release.

On a personal level, I am ultimately writing this book to give my niece and nephew a chance to have their lives back, who are both struggling with an addiction and recidivism, while at the same time help my sister get her two children back. **"True service is when helping others becomes a habit, and a true love for humanity is when you put the needs of others ahead of your own."**

The addict is like the convict that's doing a life sentence. The convict numbs himself in some way to get through the experience and to escape the reality and pain of feeling like he's going to die in prison.

The addict on the other hand loses himself in a false drug induced reality by getting high and numbing himself to escape his pain while he chases a feeling that he can never catch up to. In reality, an addict never gets high but once. After that, it's all a chase to feel something that he will never feel again, but he doesn't know that, so he chases and he chases until he becomes an addict or until he can chase no more.

In conclusion, they both are looking for an escape from something. One is running from a feeling, and the other is looking for a feeling.

But the mind can play tricks on you; the magician shows us that. Here's the trick, even after you've gotten high to escape whatever it was that you were running from, when the high wears off, it will still be there.

Before I came to prison 25 years ago, I had a favorite niece that was six years old. She was adorable; we called her Juicy. Maybe we called her Juicy because she was so sweet and plump, or maybe it was because of her plush, rash, and juicy cheeks and long hair. Whatever the reason, Juicy was a Princess.

I can remember spending hours playing with her. She laughed at almost everything. She was so much fun.

Today, I am being told by family members that Juicy is a 300lb.monster. Not long ago, Juicy took a kitchen knife and pushed it completely through one of her nieces' hand as she held her hand up as a shield to stop Juicy from stabbing her in the face.

My father who is 90 years old is totally terrified of Juicy. Like a jail, my dad has bars over his doors and windows where he locks himself in for protection from his granddaughter. Over the years Juicy has been placed in mental health institutions and the county jail.

In one day Juicy has been pistol whipped and beaten, only to return later to the same spot where she'd snatched a man's drugs and was then dragged while holding on to the drugs. This was a day in the life of Juicy. But Juicy's story doesn't end there it's only the beginning.

Juicy's tomorrow will be a repeat of her yesterday. Because Juicy is willing to risk it all to get high, but why?

I know for the prisoner that just read that says to himself, 'wow'! But Juicy's behavior is no different from someone that comes to prison, gets stabbed, is beaten, abused, extorted, sexually assaulted, and disrespected his entire prison term; is ultimately released only to return to do it all over again.

I ask the same question – 'why'?

I have a nephew who is the older brother of Juicy. My nephew is also my codefendant on my case. While I am certain that neither my niece nor my nephew is thinking of me, as I am sitting in a bathroom where I also live, writing and thinking about the both of them. I am also confident that neither of the two are thinking at all.

After serving more than 22 years of a 25-year sentence, my nephew was released from prison. Within seven months of his release he has been back before our sentencing judge on four different occasions for 'dirties.'

While my niece is struggling with an addiction, my nephew is struggling with recidivism. Consequently, at the same time my sister is struggling with the loss of her children.

INTRODUCTION

People who act like they're holier than thou are quick to pass judgment on you because they may see a flaw in you. They use the moment to treat you like a pair of old worn out shoes. They do this while forgetting that no one is perfect, and that there is no one who does not have a secret or two in their own closet.

What these holier than thou, or self-righteous individuals fail to realize is that at some point, that pair of old worn out shoes gave comfort and support to someone's feet much the same way a person who may now be struggling with a drug addiction at some gave comfort and support to someone. They could've been the beautiful daughter or the handsome son of an upstanding family or the mother and father of a beautiful son and daughter of their own. And just as the self-righteous person who is now passing judgment on you believes that they are supporting their children and providing comfort to them – although you may be struggling the moment – there was a time that you gave and provided the same kind of comfort and joy to your own children.

Despite them passing judgment on you because they choose to see you as if you have no worth, or because you look a bit worn and tattered. But instead of being able to cover up your mistakes as they do, yours just happen to be visible for the whole world to see.

You can rest assured, just as they pass judgment on you and see you as an old worn-out pair of shoes, they go through life as opportunists using people and walking on others as they do in a new pair of shoes. As soon as they've completely used that person up like a pair of shoes that they've worn, they discard them as if the person never had any value while also never realizing just how selfish and unholy they actually are.

Now we must look at the other side of this for a moment. Because it cannot be said that we have not positioned ourselves to be judged negatively if we are engaging in substance abuse.

When we engage in substance abuse we invite judgment. And when we invite this kind of scrutiny, we invite people of all ages to be just as mean as children in elementary school.

However, despite having a problem that you may be struggling with, it doesn't give anyone the right to mistreat you or treat you as if you have no worth. Just because someone has worn a pair of shoes and no longer feel that those shoes are useful, it doesn't mean that some other individual or homeless person cannot find use for them. To a homeless person that does not have a pair of shoes to place on his or her own feet at all, any pair of old shoes are just as good as new.

This is what the self-righteous, judgment-passing person doesn't realize. In the blink of an eye, you can be over your addiction or whatever crisis you may be experiencing and back to being your normal self and just as good as new, ready to provide comfort and support to others just as an old pair of shoes would be to a person who doesn't have any.

At the same time, you must be mindful that the world is full of people who want you to be nothing more than your past. When it comes to those people, you should look past them and keep on growing into the beautiful person that you are. If and when the opportunity ever presents itself for you to show judgment or generosity toward them, you should do your best to show them that you are better than they are, and that no shoes, new or used, can ever be compared to you.

You have to show them that if they are going to compare you to a pair of shoes, then they must compare you to the most durable and expensive shoes ever made because you've walked through the mud. You've passed through a construction site with the durability and toughness of a pair of steel-toed boots, and now you're back--working your magic like the glass slippers worn by Cinderella. Not those worn on the feet of a celebrity walking across the Red Carpet, but as a celebrity walking across the carpet and through it all you are still here, standing proud!

Remember, it's not those people anyway that you are living for. They will never appreciate you or your value. But like the homeless person that has no shoes, there are others who are valuable themselves that will recognize you as the beautiful human being that God created you to be and will always show you appreciation, while simultaneously respecting your worth. These are the people that matter the most. They matter the most because to them, you matter and that is what counts.

This little book depicts a story about someone that

was addicted to drugs, whose story by its end will put a smile on your face while also leaving you with a fresh desire to want what she got in exchange for her change. It will leave you with a new ambition to do what she did, and not only are you going to be inspired by the story that will leave you smiling, this book is really going to make you "think" about some things in a way that maybe you haven't thought about in a long time. Thoughts that can lead you to change the way you think. Because when you change your mind, you change your life.

Enjoy and get ready to catch yourself smiling like a kid whose just received his first toy!

WAYNE ANDERSON

1

THE AWAKENING

In 1979, for a short time, I experimented with drugs. It was the year after that I was also arrested for a crime that I hadn't committed and had absolutely nothing to do with it, but was prosecuted to the full extent of the law. Subsequently, I was sent to prison.

Nevertheless, during my prison term, something happened to me. I experienced the same kind of awakening and consciousness that I can remember experiencing when I was around the age of three.

My light clicked on. Meaning; my brain, it seems connected to the source that gives us life and intelligence. It was like sticking a plug into a socket that kick started my entire mental program, that gave me my understanding.

At that moment I became aware of my surroundings. I

realized that I was a boy, I was alive, I was riding my little tricycle, and my name was Wayne.

Ironically, in 1980, the same thing happened to me, but for a different reason.

My experimentation with drugs had done to me what it does to all of us that experiment with drugs. My drug use had put me back into a state of sleep and unconsciousness that had once again shut down my mental program, causing me to become unaware, as if I were that same little boy before I had been awakened at the age of three.

In a sense, my drug use had put me in a coma, not a medical coma, but a narcotic induced coma, that had me acting and behaving as though I was asleep. The sad thing about this state of sleep is that anyone who falls into this state of sleep, because we are still able to function in a way that allows you to still make sense of what 'you' are doing, which affords you the sense of being able to continue hustling, stealing, lying and running game to continue getting high, we deny that anything is wrong with us, in our sad state and comatosed mind. When in fact, everyone around you knows that you are dysfunctional and asleep, except you.

In a complete state of consciousness, I am aware that

there are things in this world that are far more powerful than I am; like the U.S Government, and its military, or even its judicial system and its court of law. And a drug addiction is another one. Also, in a complete state of consciousness, I would also be aware that if I am to get any help to battle these forces that are over-powering me, then it has to come from a source outside of me that's more powerful than I am.

In 1980, that source woke me up out of my state of sleep that I'd fallen into as a result of my drug use.

It's amazing, because as I see it today, it's with the same power and love- touch that we are touched with every morning that is used to awaken us out of a drug induced sleep just the same. It's like a spiritual alarm clock. Make no mistake about it, this power is 'always' there, waiting for the opportunity to wake you up. It's as close as the nearest light switch is to you, in whatever room you are in at this moment.

It's really a gift to each of us that we were allowed to wake up every morning, and even a greater gift if you are dealing with an addiction that would require you being woke, twice in the same day. Once from your natural state of sleep, and then again from your drug induced sleep.

No one, and I'll repeat that. No one wants to give you a second chance to reclaim your mind, your dignity, your appearance, and your life like this source of love that has always kept you, even in your darkest hours.

When you think back to the time that you know you were supposed to be hit by one of the flying bullets that you escaped, or the time you know you should've been sentenced to so much more time than you were given, you can even think about the   one time that you know you should've been killed, or the time you were revived from an overdose, but for some strange reason you survived every attempt on your life. If you have ever experienced anything near what I just stated, then know that a God of second chances loved you and gave you another opportunity even when you were not willing to give him 'one'!

What I personally love about this source of power that we're talking about is, it is always willing to give you a small opportunity to think, no matter what the situation is. Why wouldn't He? It's your free will to think and choose, we're not animals, we're humans. Besides, we're not robots, and shouldn't be programmed by a drug that causes us to act or behave like a robot with a habit.

In 1980, I found myself at a crossroad, but this time I was armed with a level of intelligence and consciousness that wasn't exclusively my own. I know that it wasn't my own, because at this time I also possessed a strength that I did not previously have. There, I stood in the spiritual company of something Divine that had given me the power to say no. But not the kind of NO that came across as a regular no.....it was a resounding 'NO!' that would stand forever up against any form of temptation. It was the NO that symbolized that my mind was made up. It was the kind of NO that said...."Never-Ever Again!"

From that moment until this day, I have never again experimented with drugs.

If you think being released from prison gives you a high that's nostalgic, then you ought to give yourself the chance to feel the high you get after you've been released from an addiction.

Being released myself, makes me want to see my niece be released from her addiction. I know that the Princess in Juicy is still there. She just needs to be reawakened, and upon awakening that Princess, with her moment of clarity and her split second to use her intelligence, while standing in the spiritual presence of the same God that created her to be the Princess that she was meant to be, will make a way for her to make a conscious choice as to whether or not she is going to kick her habit. The law of intelligence and its power is always standing at attention waiting for its opportunity to serve you. Intelligence never denies us the benefit of us using it. It is often times us-that denies and rejects it.

As Juicy makes a sincere declaration that she's done using drugs, this source of power that woke her up and gave her the opportunity to choose. In her moment of clarity to think for the first time in 15 years, will then release her from the self-inflicted decision of becoming an addict while transforming her back into the beautiful person that she is.

It's funny how a cartoon can have such a profound impact on children. Albeit, in this case, the impact would be on an adult. Do you remember the cartoon 'Sleeping Beauty'? Well, after being asleep for a long period of time, it wasn't until she was kissed by a knight that Sleeping Beauty was awakened. I guess in the case of Juicy, her knight would be the love touch of a God that wants to give her a second chance, and just as 'Sleeping Beauty' was awakened, Juicy, the Princess that I know and love will also be awakened.

Here's some more good news. Just as you have always got excited when you were getting high, or after you've returned from being successful from a caper, and you've got bundles of money and you wanted to share the moment with your friends, you'll have the same drive and motivation to want to share this new feeling of being free and aware, that will cause you to want to spread this love-touch over into the lives of others to touch their lives with the same touch of love that was used to change your life. And just as you once spread drugs around, you will now want to spread hope and restoration around, and my niece and nephew are the first two that I hope to restore.

I have a burning desire in me that is so strong to help them and others that I know it is not of my own will, which leads me to believe that something in the universe is assisting me in my quest and my mission to bring them back to their natural selves so they'll return back to their mother as the two children that she gave birth to , as clear-minded and loving human beings.

Life has its own way of punishing you and going against you when you go against it, and in the process, you can feel overwhelmed and unloved. Which will cause you to stop giving love or expecting to get any in return, while failing to realize that we're only getting back what we give. But given this new opportunity to start all over again new, one of the things you'll be given is a new chance to know how to love again. This is important because, we cannot seriously argue that we know how to love others. It's simply impossible to love others or yourself and use drugs at the same time.

If its love from a source that is going to be the magic that transforms you, then I would argue that this same love has to be placed back into your heart like the beat that pumps the blood through your body. Of all the virtues, love is the most powerful of them all. Whitney Houston tried to tell us that in her song, where she sang, "the greatest love of all is when you learn to love yourself." And that's the love that you must have and use to awaken others who you know and love and want to see free and unleashed from a habit or an addiction.

To love yourself, is to love your life, and when you love your life you learn to love everything about it, because you come to realize that you are connected to everything in it.

Former President Bill Clinton admitted to using marijuana. President Barack Obama also confessed to experimenting with drugs. Nelson Mandela was incarcerated for 27 years, and afterwards, he became South Africa's first Black President. And I admit to having experimented with drugs and to date I have served approximately 25 years in federal prison. Meaning, I share the past experience of each of those former Presidents. While not allowing my past to be a waste or complete period of negativity. The truth is; if it were not for my past experiences, I wouldn't be the man that I am today. As I stated previously. God it seems has always had his hand on my life, while something in the universe seemed to be assisting me. When I look back over my life today, I can see clearly now, despite my decision to delay the process, my life has unfolded and blossomed like a flower that blooms at the peak of Spring time.

Just as the experiences of Barack Obama, Bill Clinton and Nelson Mandala's experiences shaped their lives, my past experiences have done the same.

My experiences have shaped my life like a pair of masterful hands that shapes clay into an artful masterpiece. Therefore, I see no difference in their experiences from my own. My life, like yours and theirs, has always had purpose, but due to my choices, I've always interfered with that purpose, and as a result, I have delayed the outcome of my purpose.

In Barack Obama, and Nelson Mandela, I have a complete road map on how to make a difference in the lives of others while not expecting anything in return. This type of service is not only a divine act, but a supreme one.

Today, "change" is the crown that I wear proudly, while holding it high, like a trophy that's held high by a champion, while always remembering that my past is my pass into my future. At this moment I feel like I am standing in the center of the ring with both my hands being raised by the Referee, held high into the air like a Champ with two belts around my waist, having won two victories in one night. One over addiction and the other over recidivism.

2

SUCCESS IS YOUR DNA

'For that which I do, I allow not:
For what I would, that do I not;
But what I hate, is what I do.
Romans 7:15

One of the smartest things that I have ever done was to learn to ask the question, why?

Why is it that we do some of the most ridiculous and unbelievable things that we know will hurt us in the long run?

The very thing that we say that we will never do, or the thing that we know that we shouldn't do, is the exact thing we do. Even the Apostle Paul could not figure this out. Lebron James and Michael Jordan both figured it out, and now, I have, too.

Lessons do not always come from institutions of higher learning, and neither do all of the answers that we seek.

They can come from a place that you've been, or from something you've seen. They can come from life itself, or out of a book you've read. And teachers are not always people. A teacher can show up in an experience that you've had.

For me, school showed up in the vicissitude of an institution, but not one of higher learning, but in the most unsuspecting place…Behind the walls of a prison.

Although I have earned two degrees during my course of incarceration. The lessons that really educated me did not come from either the college or the University where I acquired my degrees. They came from the experience of having to live in a bathroom, while sleeping there on a bunk, with a toilet where I was forced to grow in ways that inspired me to unlearn every bad habit and erroneous thought that I previously had before coming here. Prison ultimately became, my greatest teacher.

Before I came to prison, 25 years ago, to guard my property, I purchased some of the most vicious guard dogs that money could buy. Some of these well-trained dogs can easily exceed the cost of $75,000, or more.

When purchasing these dogs, and keeping them trained, I learned a lot about life's lessons, just as I have from sleeping in a bathroom. And one of the lessons that I learned from working with these dogs, was why we do some of the things that we do, including the things that we shouldn't do. Unbelievable, but true.

When purchasing these dogs, one of the things that you look for is his ball drive, because it is with this same ball...and drive that will be used to train him, and believe it or not these dogs have so much drive and attraction to the ball that they will not only run into gun fire chasing after one, but they will run into gun fire to save your life. But this is where it gets interesting. People have the same attraction to the ball, and the same drive. Just think about it, isn't it true that law enforcement officers and soldiers engage and exchange gun fire in some situation every day? We even do it in the streets. The only difference is, dogs aren't trained with rubber balls and we are trained with fire balls (bullets).

Just think about how many different games there are in sports that involves a ball. Football, basketball, kick ball, bowling, soccer, volley ball, baseball, golf, pool, soft ball and many more games involve a ball that humans get just excited about, as the dogs are about their rubber balls. Just consider the number of fans that fill stadiums each week to see other people play with these- balls. Despite there being a growing alarm regarding brain injuries from playing football, it does not stop us from supporting the sport, nor does it stop the Athletes from playing. Obviously, the drive and attraction to play with this ball is stronger than the danger of contracting a brain injury. Now, that's something serious!

Hell, if you want to test your own attraction, just look at how excited you get when one of the teams you like scores a point, or a basket, or a goal, and if you really want to test it, just think about how you feel when you win a bet. Our attraction is so strong that we are even willing to pay someone millions of dollars just to entertain us with a ball. Is that crazy or what? No, it's just proof of how attracted we are to the ball.

So now you're saying, okay...you got me. But what does our attraction to a ball, or the attraction that the dog has to do with why we as humans do what we do. It has everything to do with it, because it's that drive that we have, it's that energy that we have, it's that rush that we get from our attraction and whenever that drive kicks in another area of our lives, Just like a fan that gets excited during a game and takes off all of his clothes and streaks across the field, when we fail to control this drive, we do stupid shit.

This drive is what influences us to do most of what we do, and if you are not conscious, you will be like the streaker at the game, but in another way. If this drive is the same drive that we get our sex drive from, then you tell me if ever, you have found yourself out of control, sexually, and if this is the same drive that propels us toward success and hard work, then explain to me where else would this drive come from. It's the same drive that we have that naturally guides us into success and into any other thing that requires energy. This is your natural gift from God, to be, and to do. The problem with this gift is that many of us misuse it, and find ourselves in trouble because we've misunderstood what is going on with us, while not realizing that, this drive is directly connected to pathways in your brain that naturally release chemicals that make us feel good so we want it and we want it all the time, and since sex triggers the release of this chemical we want it all the time. Watching or playing sports is another triggering mechanism that releases this pleasure, so sports is another one of our favorite pastimes. The pill that the addict pops, or the K2 that he smokes, or the weed that he blows, or even the opioids and heroin that he or she uses is not what makes them feel good, all of these drugs are just triggers to release the dope that they are chasing after- dopamine.

In our brains are pathways that produce a chemical called dopamine. As part of the reward-success pathway, dopamine is manufactured in nerve cell-bodies located in the ventral tegmental area of the brain, and is released in the nucleus accumbens and prefrontal cortex. I will say this, there is one absolute sure way to release this chemical, and not only will it release it, but will discharge an overflow of nothing but pure ecstasy. Just think about it. Isn't it our love for getting high, or our love for our favorite sports team that gets us pumped up? And isn't the very act of making love that takes us over the top? Love is the ultimate handle if you ever want to pull the trigger. Learn to love and you'll never have to worry about getting high again. Can you imagine having a life where everything just seems to fall into place?

Do you remember the time when we would approach the entrance of a department store and as soon as you stepped onto the mat that was laying in front of the door, it immediately opened up as if some person of royalty was about to enter the store?

What if you had a power like that, that traveled with you everywhere you went, that would open all doors, pay all bills, do all of your driving and completely protect you from all harm. You wouldn't have to worry about a thing, because you knew that everything would be taken care of.

Do you remember when Christmas was Christmas, when everybody was able to give something as well as receive? And do you remember when chivalry was the shit where real mean opened doors for women and pulled their chairs out for them? and what about this, do you remember the times when no one had automatic weapons that shot no one? How about this one, do you remember back in the 80s and 90s when we all had lots of money? I know you do, those were the days huh? Suppose you could live life like you caught the lotto? I only asked you those questions because I want you to realize that that's exactly how life is supposed to be, and believe it or not for those who has figured it out-- are living in a way as though everything is being taken care of for them. Intelligence can give you the exact life that you want. Intelligence will lead you right into your success, like a drum major leading a marching band. It's your purpose to be successful. Your passion will lead you into your purpose, and your purpose will lead you into your success.

If we can ever tap into our intelligence, we would become successful almost instantaneously.

So, you might say, I am intelligent. So why am I not successful? Because being smart is not the same as being intelligent. Smart people solve difficult math problems. Intelligent people create difficult math problems for smart people to solve.

Paul Manafort, the former Campaign chairman for President Trump was indicted in Nov. 2017 on money laundering charges, where he is accused of laundering more than $75,000,000 through off shore accounts, and spending more than a million dollars on suits alone.... Ballin!!!!! I must say, he was extremely smart, but highly unintelligent.

Smart people break the law, intelligent people prosecute them. Intelligence is what smart people chase, the way the dog chases the ball. Most all smart people envy the intelligent.

Have you ever thought about where the Rose come from? Probably not. The Rose comes from the budding petals that came from the stem, that came from the stalk, that came from the seed. Which means...the "Rose" was always in the seed. Just as our destiny to be successful is in us, our success is in our intelligence like our DNA is in our blood. Many believe that intelligence comes from institutions of higher learning. Malcom X never attended an institution of higher learning and could debate with the best of them that did go. The truth is; intelligence does not always come from our minds. For example, what if you had only one opportunity to have intelligence. Which would you rather have, the intelligence of an athlete, or the brain of a scientist? After you've answered the question, think about this.

Lebron James may not know how to solve a calculus problem, or formulate an algebraic expression, or even solve a simple algorithm. But he makes more money than any professor or mathematician that does know how to solve and calculate an algebraic expression. Lebron is intelligent in an entirely different way. Which means that many of us are intelligent in our own way, that's tied directly to what will cause each of us to be successful in our own way.

Sometimes people measure our intelligence by something we say-when in fact, our intelligence may get its best evaluation by something we do, and not by something we say.

Again, using Lebron as an example; It may appear that Lebron cannot match the intellectual wits with an English Professor, because the Professor has been trained to sound intelligent. But neither can the professor match wits with Lebron's foresight, intuition, awareness, and communication skills when he's on the court managing an entire team of athletes who all have millionaire egos. Lebron is an intellectual basketball genius.

So, intelligence cannot always be measured by what someone says. What we do is just as equally important, when compared to what someone might say that sounds intelligent.

Finally, consider this; in high school, Lebron James was as good a football player as he was a basketball player. However, his purpose was not to be a football player, he was to be the greatest basketball player of our era. And while you're considering what Lebron's purpose is, think about this. In 1995, Michael Jordan decided to give major league baseball a try. Michael soon discovered that baseball was not his purpose either, and had either Michael or Lebron chose the wrong profession, and interfered with their God-given talent and purpose. Neither would have reached the level of success that they achieved.

A perfect purpose must produce a perfect way by which to obtain, or achieve this purpose. Therefore, a perfect purpose produces perfect success.

By following their purpose, and not interfering with it by choosing the wrong sport, they both have succeeded perfectly as they should have. They both followed their intellectual drive right into success, just as you can. Success is yours. It's in your DNA.

3

MINDPOWER IS THE KEY TO INTELLIGENCE

Intelligence has power and can overcome ignorance just as light can overcome darkness. Understand that ignorance too...has power, but intelligence comes from a higher power therefore by its presence alone it can erase and replace ignorance. Aside from acquiring knowledge from an institution of higher learning there is no other game that builds mindpower and intelligence like the game of chess. Just as ice and water are of the same substance, mindpower and intelligence both exist in unity. All leaders whether they ever learned to play the game of chess or not possessed absolute mind power and intelligence. Some may have possessed intelligence that you disagree with. I would argue that it wasn't necessarily their intelligence that you disagreed with it was how they used their intelligence that you most disagreed with. Like money, intelligence answers every question, solves all problems, and is the solution to every area of your life where you need help. Therefore, the man that practices building his mindpower the most will be the man with the most intelligence. Did you know that darkness is not a thing in and of itself? It only exists in the absence of light, just as ignorance exist only in the absence of intelligence. Let us for a moment take a look at intelligence. What if some smart-aleck, non-believer asked you sarcastically why can't you walk on water as Jesus did, since you believe that you and the Savior are one, and what He did you can do also. Well, why would we want to walk on water when intelligence affords us the opportunity of riding on the water. It's because of the intelligence given to us from God that we've created boats.

Success and happiness are twin siblings of a mindpower and intelligence. But intelligence standing alone is like an elevator that can lift you up to higher levels beyond your environment.

If being uplifted is of necessity to you, then learn to see how the intellectuals of the game are playing chess with you every day.

For example; how many people when playing the game of chess can tell you what role each piece plays in a war?

What if the piece was a person or a thing?

Well, not many. Because most players never learn what the game of chess really represents. Rather than learning about the essence of the game, they play it as a recreational pastime. Most people when learning to play chess learn by first asking how each piece moves as opposed to what each piece means and because of that their next mistake is that they immediately adopt the mentality that the game is based on how they might capitalize from the mistakes of an opponent that might lead to them checkmating the king to win the game.

In chess most people think that they're outthinking an opponent when they aggressively exchange pieces as a strategy. But the best players are the ones that know how to deceive his opponent by making moves that will cause him to not only sacrifice pieces, but ultimately the game. Truthfully, chess is a strategist board for war- not a game. Prosecutors in the court of law do this every day when they over-charge defendants with additional charges to increase sentencing exposure, as a strategy to force a plea bargain, Businessmen use chess tactics every day to negotiate business deals where they come out on top. In the real war of life real chess players know the role of each piece the way a general knows the rank and role of each soldier on the battlefield, and the way every CEO knows the roles of every employee beneath him, or her. The chess players of life know that a few pieces can even be used to carry messages across the board to the king and communicate rather than be traded out. If this piece or person is used correctly, then by communicating with the king-you can learn what he is thinking. For example; in the world, just as the CIA use people to gather information, you can use a piece the way you use a spy. Rather than showing your opponent what is on your mind by allowing him to see your moves. Learn the pieces, and hide your hand. When you disguise your moves behind the moves of a piece, you hide what you are thinking and what your strategy is. Chess is an art for war that prepares you for any situation you may encounter, and at the same time it is preparing you for war, it also affords you the opportunity to build mindpower.

If you are going to be successful at learning the game to build mindpower you must consider the intelligence of others and the best way to do that is to always make it appear that their intelligence is most important. People that are egotistic only understand when they are made to feel that they are better than you are.

This move in the game of chess...softens the heart of an opponent. It removes all speculation that you have an agenda, while at the same time it places you in a position to get what you want. This move will always shine the light of generosity upon you, while making others look like the monsters they are for being inconsiderate and egotistical. You may think this to be deceptive, but people would rather have you show more interest and respect for their intelligence than be made to feel that you were out to use them. For those of us who has never learned to play the game are just common pieces. Do not feel that you have been unfair at showing one hand, but playing another. When in fact all that has happened is that you have learned how to play the game. Everyone above you has always known how to play the game. If this were not so, then the many that has authority over you would show more respect toward you, for what you are going through and your struggles. However, I suggest that you respect not only the intelligence of others but who they are as human beings. And where you have been offended by them, we should never allow our intelligence and behavior to reflect theirs. But since they fail to return the respect, it's obvious that all that matters to them is their own which simply comes down to what matters most to them. Because some people are privileged it does not mean they have the right to bully or mistreat you.

No one has the right to do you wrong, not even if wrong seems right to them. Never forget this; Whenever others see that you are always humble, respectful, poised, calm and driven by your intelligence. It draws then to you like moth to a flame. This is the move that wins trust, and can be interpreted by those around you as you being a considerate   and kind person.

During the days of prehistoric man, where was electricity, power and heat? Electricity was never created by man. It is a cause of nature. To say that man created electricity would be to say that man created lightning; and, since we know that man didn't create lightning, we know that he did not create electricity. Therefore, electricity has always been. But what hasn't always been is the level of intelligence of man to channel this source of nature into a commodity at which he could use for his own benefit. Like the Rose in the budding petal. The seed of intelligence is in you. However, like the nutrients that are needed to grow the seed that causes it to sprout. We must do that which is needed to grow our intelligence.

The Internet is a great example of how the seed of intelligence grew into a World Wide Web. In April of 1963 computer scientist J.C. Licklider wrote a memo proposing an "Intergalatic Computer Network." That October, he went to work for the US Department of Defense. There, Licklider persuaded two colleagues, Ivan Sutherland and Bob Taylor, to build a prototype network. Sutherland and Taylor had one running by the end of 1969. By 1971, fifteen computers connected to the network, by then called Arpanet.

In 1974, Vinton Cerf, Yogan Dalal, and Carl Sunshine described this growing network as "Internetworking," and used the word "Internet" for short.

In 1989, Tim Berners-Lee and Robert Caillim proposed a system where a user could click on to access information of various kind of Webs that the user could browse. This system became what we know today as the World Wide Web.

Here is an example of how we use our intelligence. Better yet; what if I set you up in a way that will help you build mindpower.

Let me ask you this. What if you were a brain surgeon and you needed to choose between these two treatments to save your patients.

Treatment "A" would save two hundred people.

Treatment "B" has a 33% chance of saving 600 and a 66% possibility of saving no one.

Which would you choose?

Well, if you chose "A" or "B", it really would not make a difference since both questions are the same. Thirty-three percent of six hundred is 200. Which means you would get the same results.

Did you see the set up?

It's like me saying to you that Stock Brokers judge the "market price by the standards of value," while regular people that buy stocks base their "standard of value on market price." Like the previous question, do you see how both groups base their judgement on "the value of a stock established by the market price?

Of course not...The Broker judges market price based on the value of the business, whereas regular investors base their judgement on the value of what the market tells them a stock is worth.

Although the second question when compared sounds exactly like the first one, in its proper context it is totally different. In fact; this was the setup, not the first question as you may have been thinking. It is not just our critical thinking that helps us to distinguish the difference in instances that appear the same, but our eyes have to be trained to see the distinction as well. Ultimately, being able to see the difference is what builds mindpower.

Consider the story told by researcher Gary Klein about a team of firefighters putting out a fire on the first floor of a house. When water was sprayed at the base of the fire, the fire didn't respond as expected - it didn't diminish at all. The chief noticed and ordered everyone out, something just didn't feel right. A few minutes later, the house collapsed, the fire had started in the basement, destroying the foundation. If it were not for the intelligence of the chief they would have been trapped inside and would've all died.

That's the power of intelligence.

Intelligence is to ignorance what light is to darkness. The difference between being intelligent and ignorant is like light and its shadow. Being ignorant is like enjoying the shadow rather than the light, when all one has to do to be intelligent is to step out of the shadow and into the light to enjoy the sunshine.

What if you could make $2 million dollars a year? Would

you like that? If you answered yes initially, that's a sign that we didn't use our intelligence. Intelligence always cautions us to question anything that sounds too good to be true and mindpower never allows us to commit to something without first investigating. Mindpower without intelligence is like thinking without a brain. Learn to build mindpower and your intelligence will serve you like a plow horse serves its master.

4

YOU MUST FIND A PSYCHOLOGY THAT WORKS FOR YOU (OTHER THAN DRUGS)

Let me explain why you have to find a psychology that will be the answer to whatever it is that you are facing, whether you 're in prison are out in society free. Imagine for me that you are in prison, a place that you definitely do not want to be to start with.

Its 6:00 AM, and the doors securing the rooms are being unlocked from the night before. Opening the doors as you would think is nothing like you would expect if you were opening the doors of your home. Once you 've unlocked the doors of your home, you probably don't give it much thought afterwards.

But inside a prison, you unlock the doors to prevent escape from some of the most dangerous men known to the world. Men who has murdered other men for money, or over disputes about money. Men who has killed other prisoners and will kill again at the first opportunity of a dispute. Men who has raped and mutilated children.

Behind these doors are men without feelings that has killed and will kill again. So, when they manufacture these locks that secure these doors, they are not ordinary locks, they are built in a way that assures prison officials that whoever they locked in the night before will be there the next morning. These locks are no less secure than the locks that are used to lock the vaults in a bank. But so much more ratchet and radical. For example; these locks operate as if there's an entire system within them that has to go through an entire process of one part releasing another part before the entire device opens. Meaning, after the officer places the key inside the lock, just turning the key is not all that happens. The key only initiates the process. Hearing one open from inside your room is like hearing someone jamming a clip into a machine gun, who then pulls the trigger releasing a single shot that has so much force and power, you cannot help but feel that the lock that was just opened was designed specifically for a wild animal or the door to a room that was securing a bomb.

This is the sound you come to expect every morning in prison that awakes you. In other words, just imagine being awakened by a gun shot every morning as your alarm clock.

Every morning at the institution where I reside starting at 6:00 AM, around the same time you hear the gun shot, you also hear an announcement that is so loud, depending upon which staff member is doing the announcement. Which will determine just how loud he or she wants to turn the volume up on the P.A. system that gives you an instant headache.

The announcement is as follows: "Notice to inmates, opposite gender staff will be working in the housing units."

This announcement rings through the intercom system so loud, either you learn to fight through the irritation, or you suffer the psychological damage that it causes. Whichever choice you make, I can assure you once you've heard the tortuous yelling of this announcement, you will never forget those words. "Notice to inmates, opposite gender staff will be working in the housing unit during the shift."

This is worse than the whip of a slave master. They whip those words across the back of your mind like an artist tattoos a drawing into the skin. It marks and scars you mentally. It reminds me of the scene in the movie Roots, where the slave master was whipping Kunta Kinte and ordering him to say that his name was Toby. To endure this announcement for years, everyday, every two hours on the hour, throughout the entire day starting with the gun shot alarm clock. Waking up to this every morning inflicts the same kind of torture and pain upon the mind that was inflicted across the back of Kunta Kinte. In addition to being shocked into consciousness every morning by the rattling of the officer's keys and the gun shot along with gender staff announcement. As soon as the doors are opened, you can be met by an officer who is dealing with his own psychological issues.

For example: recently after being shocked into consciousness, this is what followed. It happened so fast that it appeared that the officer had been waiting all night from an earlier shift for the doors to open. This particular officer has a reputation of yelling and totally disrespecting the men here. If he's not verbally abusing them, then he is constantly shining his flashlight in your face, he does this even when its day light. On this particular morning, he's in the face of a prisoner and is yelling to this adult male, excreting expletives.... 'shut the fuck up! and listen to me, shut up, don't speak.' Believe it or not, after witnessing this out burst and episode of disrespect is what inspired me to write this chapter. The officer is still yelling in the man's face and shouting, 'Shut up!' even though the man is completely silent.

He continues... 'shut up, and don't say a word, don't you talk back to me!' All of this has happened before the man had ever woke up to start his morning.

Its so bad in here that at least 75% of the men here are addicted to caffine or some other substance trying to deal with the madness. Most are over indulged coffee drinkers, drinking it to try and calm their nerves that are already on edge by the time the doors open. Its like they put your nerves at war. There couldn't be any difference if one were standing on the 100th floor of the former Twin Towers and the Planes that struck them did so on the 99th floor directly beneath you. Whatever your nerves would do in that situation is what ours is doing now.

Think about this; After you've been awake by the gun shot lock that just opened the door to your room with a frantic officer who's acting irratic and unprofessional who's standing so close to your face that it seems he spraying you with an electric paint gun of saliva and he's doing this for no legitimate reason other than him feeling that he can, while at the sametime, he expects for you to accept this mistreatment the way the slave master wanted Kunta Kinte to accept his new name.

If this were you, what would you do?

It's disheartening... -it makes your blood boil. It reaches deep down into the core of the ugliest part of who you are, well at least who you use to be, that causes you to emotionally gurgitate nothing but pure anger, resentment, and hate.

This is what I would suggest you do; you reach deep down inside of you, deep down in the same core that caused you to gurgitate the anger you feel boiling in the pit of your stomach, and use your intelligence to find a psychology (that one reason why you should think before acting.) A psychology that will cause you to understand why its more important for you to turn to something that will provide away for you to get through the experience, rather than to act out what's going through your rnind at the time.

If you think that was something, what if you were in a situation where you saw someone kill your sister, your mother, your father, and your wife, but could not do anything about it.

Wouldn't that take some serious psychology to get through?

Well, that's exactly what Dr. Frankl, a holocaust survivor had to get through during world war Il where more than six million Jews were killed by Nazi soldiers.

In Dr. Frankl's book, "'Man's Search For Meaning," he takes you inside the concentration camp where he explains the experience of being captured and forced to submit to a form of torture and slave labor that can hardly be grasped by the human mind.

He places you on the front line, on the grounds of the bestial camps where he was held captive as a prisoner, often stripped naked of his clothing with only his bare skin serving as a blanket between him and the cold ice that covered the ground where he was forced to work.

In the camps, Dr. Frankl lived like a man on death row waiting daily to be executed either by gas or the oven. In concentration camps, there were constant fighting over minuscule things like a slice of bread between men who at one time had all been successful businessmen out in society.

Dr. Frankl tells of the time after he arrived at Aushwitz

where there were more than fifteen hundred captives that were cooped in a shed that was built for no more than two hundred at the most. Freezing, cold and hungry, they had only one five-ounce piece of bread among them for four days.

There were always fights on soup day, all over a cup of water that was being called soup because it contained one or two peas at the bottom of the cup.

Once released from the sheds, the next phase was to be evaluated. If you were sent to the right, you were cleared for work, but if you were sent to the left, you were sent to the gas chambers and crematorium where you were killed almost irrnediately.

The buildings down on the left, Dr. Frankl recalled; that he was told by someone who worked down there, the word bath had been written above the doors, and as each prisoner entered the building he was handed a bar of soap, and then was allowed to stand beneath the shower head expecting a warm shower after not having one for weeks, but rather than a hot shower what they got was warm gas that left the prisoner gasping for air, as they suffocated one by one from the poisonous gas.

Dr. Frankl also remembered later that evening, he

inquired about his friend who had been traveling with him.

The response from one of the capos was, "was he sent to the left down there?" "Yes", replied Dr. Frankl.

"Then you can see him there," as the man was pointing to a dark cloud of dense smoke that was coming from the flames of a chimney, "that is your friend there, floating up to the sky", the man said.

As Dr. Frankl and others became settled into the cultural environment of camp life, they were eventually issued camp clothing. The shirt for example had to be worn for six months, until it had lost all appearance of color. For days and weeks, they could not bathe because of the frozen water pipes, and yet the sores on their hands and bodies did not suppurate unless there was frost bite.

Dr. Frankl, remembers finding himself one day at sick bay, hoping to be granted at least two days of light work inside the camp because of injuries. However, while waiting to be seen by the doctor, he stood unmoved as a twelve-year-old boy was carried past him who had been forced to work outside with bare feet because there were no shoes for him in the camp.

His toes had become frost bitten, and the doctor on duty picked off the black gangrene and infected moles from his feet tugging and pulling at them with tweezers one by one without using any anesthesia. His response to this was that he was unmoved, because he'd seen so much suffering, so many dying or the dead, that it all became common place. He even spent some time in a hut for Typhus patients who were running high temperatures. After one of them died, he watched without emotion, which was constantly repeated. One by one prisoners would approach the dead, but still warm body and remove whatever remains that were left of the dead man's food. Another his shoes, and a third his coat. Eventually, Dr. Frankl asked a nurse to remove the body. When the nurse finally decided to remove the body. He took the two feet of the dead man, pulling him from what was being used as a bed, allowing his corspe to drop several feet unto the floor making a loud solid thunk when landing hard against the floor. Then dragging it across the ground towards the door, where he had to dragg it down over sharp steps that was so high that even if you were alive and healthy it would call for you to have to raise your knees up high just to make it up the steps.

The man dragging the body approached the steps, first stepping down himself, then pulling at the feet of the dead man pulling him down over the steps until you could hear the head of the dead man drop down onto each of the steps making a loud cracking sound as it bounced against the edges of the concrete.

After seeing this, Dr. Frankl wrote the following, "Apathy, the blunting of emotions and feelings that one could not care anymore, were the symptoms arisng during the second stage of the prisoner's psychological reactions."

Although Dr. Frankl's book is more than 154 pages, that cover years of witnessing the deaths of his friends in the camps. What I just shared with you was taken from only a few pages of the book.

In my twenty-five years of a life sentence, I can identify with Dr. Frankl's experience. Sometimes we must suffer "deep" in lessons of injustice, and even so in the lessons of life, that we are taught—so that we may teach others in ways that are "deep".

A man whose life has been taken from him unjustly, who is then locked away in a room the size of a bathroom, and placed under the indefinite pressure of not knowing if he will ever have his life returned to him. His mind produces for him an experience that provides an opportunity for him to travel to a place that's so in depth and far away that his experience and insight from the experience cannot be grasped by anyone who has never been where he has been.

Thus, his lessons and teachings may be so "deep" that they come across as if they are coming out of a matrix, or somewhere in the Twi-light zone.

One of the lessons that I have learned while living in a bathroom attentatively for the rest of my life is this; **No matter how bad things may appear, your mind can 'always' be above any situation, but you have to choose this.**

In Man's Search For Meaning, Dr. Frankl asks a question. He asks, "Does the prisoner's reactions to the singular world of the concentration camp prove that man cannot escape the influences of his surroundings?"

Does man have no choice of action in the face of such circumstances?

He answers, "The experiences of camp life show that a man does have a choice. Everything can be taken away from a man but one thing, his freedom to choose."

In Dr. Frankl's search for the meaning of suffering and why he felt he had to survive was found in Logotherapy.

Logotherapy is Dr. Frankl's own version of modern

existential analysis.

This was ultimately Dr. Frankl's psychology.

To survive in my own concentration camp like experience I have studied the psychology of an amazing icon.

Although Nelson Mandela served tewenty-seven years in prison and came out to be South Africa's first black President. I needed more inspiration. I needed an underdog, I needed to study someone who were up against all the odds and won.

5

MY PSYCHOLOGY

Imagine for me that you're the owner of an Insurance company down on the eastern coast of Florida where hurricanes are prone to strike. Now consider both the risk to purchase or not purchase insurance as a customer, and the risk of insuring a customer as the owner.

Logic would dictate that if there's no pattern or record of hurricanes, then no one is probably going to buy insurance. But if we have a slew of them, as we did with Andrew, Katrina, Ivy and Maria. It can be assumed that everyone living on the coast is going to want to purchase insurance, and would also be willing to pay whatever price the owner of the insurance company wants to charge. We know this because we know their sentiments. We know their concern for property damage and the cost after a hurricane. After considering this obvious observation, you may conclude that the owner could accurately assume or

calculate how property owners will respond because....
well, when it comes down to hurricanes, that's just how
business goes. I would disagree.

Living on the eastern coast does not compel property
owners to automatically purchase insurance. Anxiety is
what forces them to purchase insurance. It's what they
think or assume about hurricanes that compels them to
secure insurance, and that's psychology- not business.

Have you ever heard of the "hardiness" research studies
done by the International Committee for the study of
victimization? These studies looked at people who had
suffered serious adversities. For instance; people who had
been imprisoned such as Dr. Frankl, cancer survivors,
victims of serious accidents, victims of mass shootings,
victims of molestation and etc. What they discovered was
subjects of this research generally fall into three distinct
categories: Those who were permanently marred from the
experience, those who were able to pull their lives back
together after the experience, and those who used the
experience as a defining moment that pushed them to
higher heights that ultimately brought the best out of them.

Oprah Winfrey is just the person described in category
three. Oprah was born into poverty in rural Mississippi to

a teenage single mother and later raised in an inner-city Milwaukee neighborhood. As a child Oprah was molested by a cousin and a friend of the family. Whenever you molest a child, you scar them. You violate their human rights, and their right to choose not to be touched. You leave them with a memory that will forever be tattooed into their minds, like the death of a parent. We should 'respect' and 'protect' children, not touch them.

As a teenager Oprah became pregnant, but lost her son in infancy. This would add even more stress and hardship on her. Oprah's mother traveled with her where she spent her first six years living in rural poverty with her maternal grandmother, Mrs. Hattie Mae (Presley) Lee who was so poor that Oprah often had to wear dresses made of potato sacks. She was often the laughing stock of the class and made fun of by other students at school. She lived through the experience of losing two half-sisters due to Aids-related causes and causes related to cocaine addiction. At the age of thirteen, because of the abuse she ran away from home. Considering what seemed to be a bleak, if not sordid and horrific script that was written for her life, who would have guessed that the Oprah Winfrey that we know today could've come from such a tumultuous beginning.

Here's what happened. Oprah found her psychology.

She allowed her past experiences to teach her. Her hurt, her suffering and pain became the GPS that directed her to the school that would become her greatest teacher. Rather than break, and put her head under the sand. She used her past to build a career on top of the same sand that she could have just as easily have buried her head in. She certainly had all of the embarrassing reasons to shun the public, or to become a public figure.

But right in line with the study that was conducted by the International Committee for the study of Victimization, she used what should have destroyed her as an opportunity to redefine herself, and who she became was an Icon. Known today as the Queen of media, she is the richest African-American and North America's first black Billionaire. She has been awarded the Presidential medal of Freedom by President Obama, and honorary degrees from Duke and Harvard.

From 2006 to 2008, because of her influence, her endorsement of Obama delivered over a million votes. Oprah has owned the title of being the most highly celebrated talk show host in the history of America.

While we may know Oprah for her philanthropic

contributions and business acumen, at heart and by example: she's a proficient and skilled teacher. She is an excellent teacher because she has been an excellent student of her past experiences. From them she has found a way to duplicate what she learned to teach others how to get the most out of their past experiences while empowering them with the same mantra that she has used to help her get through her own tumultuous times.

As a leader, sometimes, it's not about how much you know, or how well you can lead with your vision. Sometimes, it's about giving those around you or those who are following you the power to help you lead by asking them the right questions.

Oprah's grandmother once said that ever since she could talk as a child, she played games interviewing her corncob dolls.

Watching Oprah embrace her past while standing up against the brutal facts of her experiences, and conquering them the way David conquered and slew Goliath. I have stood in the face of a judicial giant that has placed me in a bathroom to live out the remainder of my life for a non-violent drug offense. However, despite having been dealt this unfortunate hand, I must remain sane. A feat that hasn't been easy.

But what I learned from Oprah was that I could use my experience to make me better, not bitter and rather than allow my current condition to define me, instead I could use it to re-define myself, and that was to come out of this being the best person that I could be. It has been a psychology that has gotten me through and will get you through whatever rough spot in life that you think you may have. The power to overcome any obstacle is within you.

As a student of this psychology, I have always remained persistent, uncompromising and driven.

Remember: no matter how bad things may appear, your mind can always be above any situation, but you have to choose this. Over the past twenty-five years that I have spent living in a bathroom where I naturally have a toilet. Also have my eating table there as well. Who eats where they also defecate? This is inhumane. And it's this psychology that gets me through. I've chosen to allow my mind to always be higher than any predicament and situation. You always have a choice regarding who you will be in any situation.

There is nothing aside from brute force that is more powerful than humility, poise, calm, consistency, and your drive to survive and overcome.

In the sixties, Dr. King displayed those exact attributes that ushered black America into desegregation and the civil rights Act of 1964. That's power! With those attributes we overcame Jim Crow.

Though I'm aware that we still have work to be done, but by the grace of God, we've had: the opportunity because of our drive to persist, to see America's first black president because of leaders like Dr. King, Oprah and Barack Obama.

In addition to Oprah's drive to be the best at what she does, would you agree that Oprah was blessed with the gift of vision, that allows her to see things from a higher perspective that's higher than normal.

She has a unique way of seeing things, and then communicating what she sees in a way that is clearly understood by others whom she also teaches to see as she does while interviewing.

Her unique vision affords her the skill to see from the top-down (sort of like an Eagle) through the clouds into the bright light of truth. Her gift allows her to see completely through the eyes of millions. Therefore, making it possible for her to know what millions desire collectively.

She knows there will never be a single movement that galvanizes America in its totality. So, she has embarked upon a career that allows her to reach out to America one interview at a time, one production, one broadcast at a time to unite America.

She has mastered the Art of teaching people how to see things in a way that moves them towards their own goals, and their desire to succeed. More so, towards their own higher calling.

She does this so masterfully, that it almost comes across as being magical. It's one thing to be intelligent and have full function of your mental faculties, but quite another if your eyes are wide open and out of focus, and you have a hearing deficit when it comes down to being conscious and in tune with truth.

Whenever Oprah is interviewing, she uses the moment to teach. She uses the opportunity to galvanize a disenfranchised and divided population of people. She uses her platform to always tailor her questions to get the best answers for audiences that need the same answers, and to do that on a world scale is a gift.

She's so good at what she does, in some instances she could be interviewing about a topic that we are totally disinterested in, but because of her skill; we find ourselves fully emerged by her ability to ask the right questions or we find ourselves mesmerized by her techniques rather than by the information that she extricated from the question. Seeing Oprah interview is like seeing Michael Jordan slam a basketball for the win in NBA championship final, when you understand what she is doing.

Imagine Oprah closing out this chapter of the book. For the precise purpose of what we're trying to get across. I can hear her pose the following question. 'How many of you would say that my success in business all started from my talk show?'

I would be surprised if not everyone that was asked that question would not agree with her based on how she asked the question. However, I would disagree. Oprah's success came from her learning from her chaotic beginning, that motivated her to redefine herself.

Oprah found her psychology. She found what worked for her, while simultaneously, it got her through. It brought her out of a tumultuous past, where she found her passion for doing something she was good at. Allowing her past to teach her, she learned, then mastered the art of communicating and asking the right questions that reached the largest number of people who were all interested or in need of the same answer. She did this so well that even if you had none that were interested in the answer, they still found her way of asking the question entertaining.

Her ability to cause one to see in ways they've never seen, or to give one a voice that has never before been heard, and the opportunity to think in a way they've never thought, is what took Oprah to the top, and that's psychology. That's skill, not business. Business is just the by-product of what she does. Her success stemmed from discovering who she was and what she was good at.

If Oprah's success has come from her finding her psychology (using her past to motivate her to want better) then imagine what finding your psychology will do for you.

At the beginning of a tumultuous beginning, or in the middle of a chaotic journey, we all need a 'healthy' psychology that will bring us success, or carry us through our journey of turmoil. The death of a loved-one requires a psychology. A divorce. News of a terminal illness. The loss of a job. Molestation and rape. Depression, Racism, Bigotry, Abandonment, Addiction, Alcoholism. The simple act of living; alone is enough to need a psychology.

This is what I know. If you ever want to experience

power, and success. Find a psychology that is perfect for you, and you will have found your answer.

Let your psychology be the perfect answer to the question that Oprah would ask you. What are you waiting on?

6

YOU WERE BORN TO BE SUCCESSFUL, UNADDICTED AND FREE!

'And Jesus immediately knowing in himself
that virtue had gone out of him, turned
and said, who touched me?'

Mark 5:30

When someone inspires you, at that very moment God has given you the power to become whatever you want to become.

We know what happens when you touch Jesus, but what happens when God touches you?

When you've been inspired by someone, you become the embodiment of whoever that person is, and take from them whatever they have.

For example: If you take a drop of water from the ocean, is it not in fact the ocean, of course it is not the entire ocean, but it is everything that the ocean is, because it comes directly from its source, and therefore is everything that it comes from.

When the woman with the issue of blood touched Jesus, she took from Jesus some of what he had. She took enough of his power to heal herself.

Whenever you feel inspired, that's the spirit of God giving you everything you need to accomplish everything you want.

A lot of the men here, including prison officials call me, 'Tyler Perry.' Although I do not see myself as Tyler. How can I? But I must admit that its rather flattering to be compared to one of the greatest Playwrights, and successful Directors of our era. Tyler's success is a dream come true.

After Watching Tyler   Perry's plays, I was inspired by his genius to be able to make people laugh, while having a good time. In that, I saw the perfect opportunity to teach others in prison how to go home and be successful, while making them laugh. No prisoner that has ever worked with me in the play that was released, has ever returned to prison.

Tyler Perry has no idea that I, like the woman that

touched Jesus' clothes, I've touched his.

What I took from Tyler when I touched his craft, is what people see when they see one of my plays. Therefore, I assume this is why they call me, Tyler Perry. Like the drop of water taken from the ocean. When I write, direct and act in these plays, I become everything that Tyler is.

When Tyler Perry inspired me, God gave me what he'd placed in Tyler. Inspired by him, my name is now known throughout all 122 federal prisons because of the content and success of these plays. The plays are so impactful, that not only does the prison allow me to present them to the children that come here to visit with their families, but I have had the rare opportunity of meeting and/or have interacted with five different Directors of the BOP, including officials from the Obama Administration. This is what happens when you've been inspired. Inspiration happens for two reasons only; to bless you and to change your life.

Just as I have written this book to inspire change in the lives of men who are struggling with addiction and recidivism. I write the plays to teach the men while preparing them to make successful transitions back into society.

Whenever someone inspires you, you can rest assure that your life is about to change.

At the time I was inspired by Tyler, it was as if something inside of me was saying, 'make a wish.' I did, and everything I hoped to become, I became.

Now that I have the gift to inspire others to become successful, if I can inspire Juicy, at that very moment, I know that she will lose her appetite to use drugs, while she gains her appetite to use drugs. I know that was confusing. Let me explain; When Juicy loses her appetite to continue using drugs to get high, she'll gain the appetite to use her drug experience to inspire others to lose their appetite for using drugs, meaning, the same love that she once had for getting high will be the same love that she has for teaching others not to get high.

If I had just one more wish, it would be to help my niece overcome her addiction. Juicy deserves to live before she dies. No one that has been addicted to drugs all of their adult lives have ever lived. Because of my concern for her I constantly live in fear that one day I will be notified to call home for that one emergency call that Juicy's life has been cut short and that she's been found behind some abandoned building murdered in the most gruesome way.

In October, 2017, I received a message that I needed to call home right away. I braced for the news that I have always feared. I made the call; while listening to the recording, I waited for my dad to answer the phone. In the feds you can't just dial straight through, there is always a recording that gives the receiving party the chance to either accept or reject your call. As always, because my dad is slow to press the 5, the recording is now repeating itself, "Your call is now being processed, pause....when the person on the receiving end picks up, a second part of the message starts to play,' you have a prepaid call from (whoever is calling) you will not be charged for this call, this call is from a federal inmate to accept the call press 5."

My dad finally accepted the call. After exchanging our pleasantries, he paused.

I knew it was coming. When he did speak, he said, "'Your friend is back in jail with 12 charges and no bond."

Because my mind had been set to hear something about Juicy, I totally missed what he said.

"I'm sorry pop's, I said. Repeat that."

"Your friend is back in jail."

I have a friend by the name of Daryl Smith that was recently released from prison after doing 24 years. My love for this friend is more like that of a brother, I love him dearly. Hearing this news reminded me of why I wrote this book in the first place, or why I write the plays. To help other men not reoffend. Hearing this news was more personal to me than just hearing that my friend was back after doing 24 years, because I am now in my 25th year I know the pain that he must have been feeling to be back. Due to the pain that I am now feeling, I could not imagine what he must have been feeling, this feeling has to be like being at your own funeral while you are completely conscious.

In the medical field there is proof that sleep deprivation will kill you if you do not get any sleep within a certain number of hours. I am not aware of the exact amount of time lost that will cause injury or death, but what I do know is that I have gone almost five days without closing my eyes.

After finally digesting this information from my dad and was about to end the call, he said, "wait son, I have something to tell you."

My dad is an older guy, 90 to be exact, so I assumed that maybe he'd forgotten just that fast that he had already told me about my friend.

He said, "Son the doctors ran tests on me and they found a mass of something in my stomach."

I know what my dad had said to me, and I know what he thought I heard, but nothing could have been further from the truth. What he said and what I heard was totally different. What I heard was my pop's trying to tell me is that he had cancer without telling me that he had cancer. Since I've been in, I have already lost my mother, and now this. At that moment I felt like dropping the phone and giving up, but I remembered   how I have always taught the men around me to always stay poised and push through any situation that they encounter, and so I did just that.

He interrupted the pause. "By the way," he said. "Juicy is over here, but I don't think she'll know who you are, she's in pretty bad shape."

Before I could even fix my mouth to speak, before I knew it, I beckoned him to put her on the phone. As Juicy was reaching for the phone, I timed it perfectly, like a quarterback timing his receiver on an out route.

Just as the quarterback throws the perfect pass, as soon as I felt that Juicy could hear my voice, the first thing I said was, "I love you."

She never said a word. For the next five minutes, she

cried. I never interrupted her while she cried. I could tell that crying was something she needed to do. After she'd released all of her pain through her tears, she finally spoke. She said, "Uncle Wayne, I love you too."

I said to her, if I ever come home that she was coming with me and that I was going to help her.

In return she said, "okay."

With that being said, we ended the call.

Over the next four and a half days from this one phone call, I would not get one wink of sleep.

When I finally closed my eyes, shortly after, something woke me up. Whether it was a dream I do not know, but whatever it was, it spoke to me, saying, "You inspired Juicy to change."

After speaking with Juicy that day, I would continue to send her letters encouraging her and sharing with her how I'd turned my life around and letting her know about all the great things that I was doing with my life.

Then, out of nowhere one day, I received a letter from her with the beginning of a manuscript that she had began writing. It was the preamble of her children's book. With a little love and inspiration, Juicy had gone from being a crack addict to now becoming an Author. The book was about a little boy and his grandparents teaching him about work.

This is what she wrote:

Title: "Idris" (The Little Boys Name), My first job!

Hi my littlepreneur friends! Its time to watch and learn all about your first job. It's time for school, said Idris....'Grandma, do you have me all packed and ready to go?' 'Grandpa, are you coming with me to?'

'No son, off to work I go.... see you when I return'.

'Hmmm? ....WORK?'

Idris wonders what's that all about. Then he says,

'Papa, can I go to work?'

'Sure son, your first day of training has just begun, now get on to school before you're late for work, see you when you return', chuckles Grandpa.

So, while Grandma and Idris heads to school Idris asks, 'do you have to work too Grandma?'

'Of course, Grandma responds...grandma has to make sure the family business is kept good.'

Well alright, in that case, guess you best to hurry and get me to school so I don't be late for my work, right Grandma?'

'That's right son...papa's lil-handyman'!

'Your teachers will be waiting on their best little worker to report to class. You do want to learn and earn huge rewards right Idris?'

'Yes mam, of course I do!'

'Hurry Granny, look...my desk, I've got work to do. Are my crayons in my bag?'

'Yes Idris, but wait, here comes your teacher now. Say good morning to Ms. Tamara.'

'Good morning Mrs. Tamara,' Idris shouts!

Grandma then turns to leave and waves good bye. Idris turns to his teacher excited because of what grandpa told him about the rewards of working.... he then tells his teacher, 'I am here to work!'

He holds up his drawing that he has to paint (as she is teaching him his colors) then he thinks.... mmmm...papa said I'll need my tools. Now where are my tools Idris began to search.... oh yeah, lets' look inside my back pack. He then reaches and pulls out his crayons.......after painting his drawings...he learns his numbers and he receives a treat as a reward for learning to count from both the school and his grandpa who pays him in coins and teaches him how to save them and start an account. The second day of school, Idris gets up super-excited yelling to his grand-parents that it's time to go to work.

Granny says, 'no... you're going to school.'

'No Granny, Idris responds.... I'm like Grandpa, I'm going to work. I have to learn to earn so I can take care of the family like Grandpa. Grandma, do you have my back pack ready?'

Grandpa said always make sure you report to work with all the proper tools, because if I don't, I will not be able to earn my best reward.

After the first week of school, Idris was excited about showing granny his grades. As soon as his Grandma picked him up from school Idris began yelling,

'Look Grandma, this is my reward card, I am doing my best, see I got A's and papa said it helps him with his work when he gets good marks, and whenever I do it, he gives me $1.00 for each "A" that I get. Let's count how many A's I got grandma. I got five A's, 5 A's...wow! Grandma....I earned $5 dollars.'

After reading the beginning of Juicy's book, there was no doubt in my mind that through showing her love, that I had inspired her, and now she wanted to inspire children.

Inspiration and a little love turned Juicy's entire life around.

What if Juicy's book could inspire your child?

What if one day you asked your son or daughter how was their day in school, and in response they said to you.

'You owe me $5.00.'

And you ask, how is that?

And they tell you because Idris' grandpa gives him $1.00 for each 'A' that he gets.

'I've got five A's on my reward card, so you owe me $5.00.'

How would that make you feel?

I told you this book would make you feel good.

ABOUT THE AUTHOR

Wayne Anderson is a federal prisoner incarcerated since September 13, 1993. He is serving a life sentence for a non-violent offense. Currently, he is working as a clerk in the vocational Training and Educational Department at the Federal Correctional Complex-Medium where he's worked as a clerk for the vocational and Educational Department for approximately four (4) years.

Prior to working as an educational clerk, Wayne worked for the Federal Prison Industries, Inc. (UNICOR) at the United States Penitentiary Atlanta as an Accountant technician, overseeing an entire warehouse of merchandise known as SST1.

Wayne is certified in a variety of areas, such as computer programs. He's certified in the Microsoft Office Suite which includes Excel, Word, PowerPoint and Access. He's also certified in System Application Product (SAP), which is commonly referred to as Millennium; an official record keeping integrated manufacturing, accounting software package and management information system.

Wayne has created and innovated programs for the Bureau of Prisons; such as Fathers Rebuilding Bridges program; Mothers Rebuilding Bridges for the women Camp; the first ever Spanish Threshold class (a spiritual based program for Hispanics); the Re-entry and Rehabilitation Movement; He co-authored the curriculum for the Bridge to Re-entry; he has also served as a mentor in the Skills program where he was paired up with mentally challenged inmates as a Mental Health Companion.

Wayne is the innovator for one of the most highly recognized programs in the Bureau of Prisons called the Re-entry Theatre Group.

Since incarceration Wayne has earned two separate degrees, an Associate's Degree in business with honors from Ashworth College, and only a few credit's shy of receiving a Bachelor's of Arts from Adams State University. Wayne has also learned to speak Spanish, while also studying Portuguese, and the Italian language.

Wayne is a humble spirit, who lives by Christian principles. He prides himself with knowing that today he is truly a rehabilitated human being who serves God and humanity with a passion.

"True service is when serving others become a habit."

- Wayne Anderson

Please visit us at:

www.afmpublishers.com

for other books we have available as well as all the other services we offer.

www.ingramcontent.com/pod-product-compliance
Lightning Source LLC
Chambersburg PA
CBHW022125280326
41933CB00007B/552